The Delano GRAPE STRIKE

BY DANIEL MAULEÓN

ILLUSTRATED BY JÁNOS ORBÁN

CONSULTANT:

JAMES ZARSADIAZ

ASSOCIATE PROFESSOR OF HISTORY

DIRECTOR, YUCHENGCO PHILIPPINE STUDIES PROGRAM

UNIVERSITY OF SAN FRANCISCO

CAPSTONE PRESS

a capstone imprint

Published by Capstone Press, an imprint of Capstone.
1710 Roe Crest Drive, North Mankato, Minnesota 56003
capstonepub.com

Library of Congress Cataloging-in-Publication Data
Names: Mauleón, Daniel, 1991– author. I Orban, Janos, illustrator.
Title: The Delano grape strike / by Daniel Mauleón ; illustrated by Janos Orban.
Description: North Mankato, Minnesota : Capstone Press, [2023] I Series:
Movements and resistance I Includes bibliographical references and index. I
Audience: Ages 8–11 I Audience: Grades 4-6 I Summary: "On September 16, 1965,
Filipino and Mexican American migrant workers joined together to strike against
the grape growers in Delano, California. The farmers left the
fields to demand better wages and benefits. Led by Larry Itliong, Cesar Chavez,
and Dolores Huerta, the two groups created a union called the United Farm
Workers of America. For five years, UFW brought attention to their cause through
boycotts, a 300-mile march, and other nonviolent efforts in what became an
important victory in the fight for labor and farmworker rights in the
United States"—Provided by publisher.
Identifiers: LCCN 2021054241 (print) I LCCN 2021054242 (ebook) I
ISBN 9781663959225 (hardcover) I ISBN 9781666322934 (paperback) I
ISBN 9781666322927 (pdf) I ISBN 9781666322972 (kindle edition)
Subjects: LCSH: Grape Strike, Calif., 1965–1970—Juvenile literature. I Vineyard
laborers—California—Juvenile literature. I Migrant agricultural laborers—
California—History—Juvenile literature. I United Farm Workers of America—
History—Juvenile literature. I Agricultural laborers—Labor unions—California—
History—Juvenile literature. I Chavez, Cesar, 1927–1993—Juvenile literature.
Classification: LCC HD5325.V52 1965 M38 2023 (print) I LCC HD5325.V52 1965
(ebook) I DDC 331.5/4409794—dc23/eng/20220217
LC record available at https://lccn.loc.gov/2021054241
LC ebook record available at https://lccn.loc.gov/2021054242

Editorial Credits
Editor: Christopher Harbo; Designer: Tracy Davies; Media Researcher: Svetlana
Zhurkin; Production Specialist: Katy LaVigne

All internet sites appearing in back matter were available
and accurate when this book was sent to press.

TABLE OF CONTENTS

LARRY ITLIONG AND THE MANONGS

The history of farm labor in the United States is laced with oppressive working conditions. It started in the 17th century when slavers took Africans by force from their homeland and brought them to work against their will on plantations.

After the 13th Amendment to the U.S. Constitution ended slavery in 1865, unfair farm labor continued. Throughout the 19th century, workers from China and Japan came to the United States. They did backbreaking work for very little pay.

In the mid-1800s, Mexican migrant workers began crossing the border to work farm fields around the country. By the 1920s, more than 150,000 farmworkers in the United States were either Mexican or Mexican American.

Around the same time, another group of laborers began coming to the United States.

Between the 1920s and 1930s, more than 100,000 Filipino men immigrated from the Philippines. They heard money could be made in America, so they sold their belongings to pay for travel across the ocean.

But when they arrived, they discovered the working conditions were harsh. They spent 10 or more hours a day hunched over in the heat, and the farm growers wouldn't provide bathrooms or water on work sites. In addition, their wages were so low they couldn't afford to travel back to the Philippines.

How long can we work like this?

What other choice do we have?

Many of these Filipino workers ended up living at labor camps run by the growers. The shacks were worn down, workers had to share rooms, and the outhouse stalls were not maintained.

In addition, Filipino workers—like many immigrant workers before them—faced discrimination and racism. They didn't have the right to vote, and they couldn't own property or businesses.

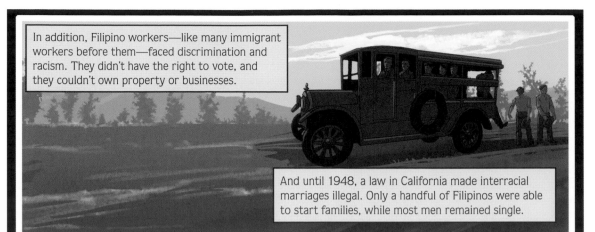

And until 1948, a law in California made interracial marriages illegal. Only a handful of Filipinos were able to start families, while most men remained single.

Season after season, these men worked and lived together. To the younger Filipinos who came to the United States in the 1940s and 50s, the older generation became known as the Manongs—a word meaning older brother, or elder.

Without homes and families, the Manongs became migrant workers who traveled north along the West Coast from farm to farm. Each season, they harvested grapes in California, picked apples and lettuce in Washington state, and canned salmon in Alaska. Then they would return south to follow the same cycle year after year.

San Francisco

Delano

Los Angeles

Coachella

In 1929, 15-year-old Larry Itliong was one of the thousands of Filipinos who immigrated to the United States.

He hoped to get a formal education and become a lawyer. To earn money, Itliong became a migrant worker.

Like other migrant workers, Itliong followed the work wherever it took him. Along the way, he became interested and involved in the rights of workers.

Unity is strength!

He joined his first labor strike in 1934 alongside lettuce workers in Washington. Later, he co-founded the Alaska Cannery Workers Union, which successfully fought for a contract for an eight-hour workday with overtime pay.

By the mid-1940s, Itliong settled in Stockton, California. There he partnered with fellow Filipino Philip Vera Cruz to establish the Agricultural Workers Committee (AWOC).

We can fight for better wages, but we need to fight for better living and working conditions too!

This group worked with the American Federation of Labor and Congress of Industrial Organizations (AFL-CIO) to create better working conditions for its members.

In May 1965, Itliong and the Manongs were about to begin another season on the grape farms in Coachella Valley, California. They asked for an increase in wages to keep up with living expenses. They wanted $1.40 per hour*, which was a 15-cent-an-hour raise from the previous season. It was also the rate the Mexican workers were getting through a federal program.

Every farm we have worked this year has given us our due raise.

Your people will work for a dollar twenty-five or you won't work at all!

*$1.40 in 1965 equals about $11.68 today.

But the growers at Coachella refused their demands.

By this time, some of the Manongs were in their 50s and 60s. Retirement was just around the corner, and they needed every cent they could make.

So when the Coachella growers refused to increase wages, Larry Itliong and the AWOC led the Manongs in a strike.

Nearly 1,000 Filipino workers joined the Coachella strike, and their tactic quickly paid off. After 10 days, the growers gave in to their demands for fair wages.

Enough, enough! You will get your one dollar and forty cents an hour.

By September, the Manongs and other Filipino workers moved farther north. They arrived at the grape farms of Delano, California, in time for the harvest and were offered $1 an hour.

San Francisco

Delano

Los Angeles

Coachella

As they had in Coachella, the workers asked for a raise to $1.40 per hour. Once again, the growers refused.

Even in Coachella, they listened and gave us one-forty.

Well, we do things differently in Delano. We've got plenty of people willing to work for less.

WALKING OFF THE FIELDS

On September 7, 1965, Itliong and Vera Cruz gathered the Manongs and other Filipino workers at the Filipino Hall in Delano. The AWOC was taking another strike vote.

Once again, the older Manongs needed every penny they could earn and save for retirement. They felt confident because of their successful strike in Coachella just a few months before.

During the meeting, Itliong reminded the workers why they should strike.

We work all day in the heat. The growers do not provide bathrooms or water. And if anyone gets injured, we have no health care, no insurance.

I want those in favor of striking to stand up with your hand raised.

It was a unanimous decision. They were going on strike.

The very next day, the workers arrived at 3:00 in the morning for their normal shift at the grape farms.

As always, they began by cutting grapes off of the vines and leaving them at the base of the plant.

Then, before the workers would normally begin collecting the grapes, about 2,000 Filipinos walked off the farms.

The Delano Grape Strike had begun.

The Filipino workers spent the first week of the strike picketing outside of farms. They demanded higher wages and better conditions in the fields and in their camps.

We are your brothers and sisters over here! Come on out!

They also tried to talk any replacement workers—known as scabs—into leaving the fields and joining the strike.

Meanwhile, the growers were not happy and quickly tried to break the strike.

We won't be intimidated!

They hired security to harass and assault the picketers. Some even sprayed the strikers with pesticides.

And the growers didn't limit their actions to the picket lines. Since the strikers lived in labor camps near the farms, the growers lashed out there as well. To punish the workers, they cut the water, gas, and electricity in their homes.

But the growers' most reliable tool for breaking the strike was a highly effective strategy they had used in the past. They pit one group of farmworkers against another.

With the Filipino workers on the picket line, the growers paid the Mexican workers just a little more to take over the job.

We're going to need the support of the Mexican workers for the grape strike to work.

As a result, Itliong went to the National Farm Workers Association (NFWA). This farm labor union was mostly made up of Mexican American members.

The NFWA was led by Mexican American labor leaders César Chávez and Dolores Huerta. Chávez had worked as a laborer and served in the Navy before becoming a labor leader.

Huerta had been an elementary teacher who had seen firsthand how the children of migrant farmers were affected by poverty.

Together, Chávez and Huerta had co-founded the NFWA in 1962.

HARVESTING SUPPORT

When Itliong first approached the NFWA to join the strike, Chávez declined.

Itliong knew he couldn't wait any longer, and he wasn't about to back down.

If you don't join us now, we won't help you when you finally do strike. We need to do this together, and now is our best chance.

Itliong's persistence, along with growing brutality from the growers, finally convinced Chávez and Huerta to take action.

On September 16, they gathered the NFWA members at the Our Lady of Guadalupe Church in Delano to vote on joining the strike.

During the meeting, the Mexican workers heard arguments for and against joining the Filipinos on the picket line. At long last, the vote was taken, and chanting erupted inside the church.

¡Si se puede! [Yes, we can!]

¡HUELGA! ¡HUELGA! ¡HUELGA! [STRIKE!] [STRIKE!] [STRIKE!]

The following Monday—September 20, 1965—the members of NFWA joined the picketing members of AWOC, and the labor movement grew. In August 1966, the two unions would merge into the United Farm Workers Organizing Committee, which would later become the United Farm Workers union (UFW)

DELANO GRAPE STRIKERS AWOC AFL-CIO

HUELGA NFWA

HUELGA NFWA

HUELGA NFWA

HUELGA NFWA

HUELGA NFWA

Unlike the 10-day Coachella strike, the Delano Grape Strike ended up lasting years. But as time went on, the Filipino and Mexican strikers gained support in many different ways.

Throughout the strike, Itliong, Chávez, and Huerta all worked hard to drum up support for their cause.

Itliong traveled across the country speaking to college students and organizations. His goal was to raise awareness and money for the UFW and its striking members.

The grapes from your dining halls are picked by the workers in Delano under terrible working conditions and low wages. The workers deserve better, and they need your help!

On March 17, 1966, Chávez and about 75 other strikers started a march from Delano to Sacramento, California's state capital. They visited communities along the way to share their story.

On April 10, the march arrived in Sacramento. Chávez addressed a crowd of nearly 8,000 people. The 340-mile march was a success and raised awareness for the UFW's movement across the country.

Sacramento

NEVADA

CALIFORNIA

340 miles!

PACIFIC OCEAN

Delano

MEXICO

WESTERN UNION TELEGRAM

LB23 AB275

A LLV232 PDB 1 EXTRA=FAX ATLANTA GA 5 303P EST=
CESAR CHAVES, UNITED FARM WORKERS=
P O BOX 130 DELANO CALIF=

You and your fellow workers have demonstrated your commitment to righting grievous wrongs forced upon exploited people. We are together with you in spirit . . .

It even drew the attention of civil rights leader Dr. Martin Luther King Jr., who sent a telegram to Chávez.

In 1967, Huerta enlisted the help of Mexican women to lead another boycott. Banding together, they picketed grocery stores and encouraged ordinary citizens to stop buying grapes from farms the UFW was striking against.

FOOD MARKET

Boycott Grapes! Boycott Grapes!

Because most shoppers couldn't track which farms their grapes came from, many people stopped buying California table grapes altogether. This, in turn, added new pressure on the Delano growers as they faced anger from other California grape growers who were losing money.

Before long, many organizations began offering their support to the UFW's cause as well.

The National Association for the Advancement of Colored People (NAACP) passed out flyers encouraging shoppers across the country to support the strikes.

can your family live on less than $1800 a year?

Packing plant workers in California refused to package grapes.

Take your grapes somewhere else--we support the grape workers here.

The Student Non-Violent Coordinating Committee (SNCC) of California wrote about the strike in their paper. They also provided two-way radios to help strikers track down and discourage scab workers.

We support your movement, and hopefully these radios will help you out.

The Black Panther Party (BPP) partnered with the UFW to boycott Safeway, one of the largest grocery store chains on the West Coast.

THERE'S BLOOD ON THE GRAPES

grapes & lettuce

Let's help you find a better place to buy your food.

In addition to picketing outside stores, BPP members offered Safeway shoppers rides to and from other grocery stores that supported the boycott.

As the strike and boycott grew, they drew praise and criticism from many political and public leaders.

Senator Robert Kennedy, who served on a U.S. Senate labor committee, visited Delano several times ahead of his run for president.

We're going to try and improve not just your lives, but more importantly the lives of your children.

Meanwhile, Ronald Reagan, who was the governor of California, held very different feelings about the grape boycott. He was often seen eating grapes in opposition to the movement.

The grape boycott? I believe it to be immoral.

As a former actor, Reagan's negative experiences with the actors' union led him to believe unions were full of corruption. To him, the UFW was just another corrupt union hurting workers.

Although the pressure on growers to improve working conditions and wages was mounting, they refused to give in.

When they couldn't get local workers to farm their fields, they brought workers in from far away. And even though it was illegal, they also brought in workers from Mexico who were unaware of the strike.

But busing in laborers was expensive. So to save costs, the growers often paid these replacement workers even less than the local workers who had gone on strike.

As a result, many of the replacement workers walked off the fields and joined the strike too!

This is ridiculous!

The ongoing problem of finding and keeping replacement workers was compounded by the growing challenges to sell their crops. To get around the grape boycotts in the United States, growers started shipping their product to Canada and Europe.

But in Montréal, Canada, activist Jessica Govea led another boycott. With marches and leaflets, she discouraged Canadians from buying California table grapes.

And in London, England, members of Britain's largest union refused to unload the grapes and left them to rot on the boats.

You can send those grapes back. They aren't welcome here.

Soon, the strike the Manongs started in Delano grew into an international movement for workers' rights—and the growers reached a breaking point.

VICTORY AND DEFEAT

Finally, almost five years after the strike began, the growers buckled to the pressure. It took two weeks of negotiations, but on July 29, 1970, the UWF and 26 growers signed their first farming labor contract.

Thanks to everyone who helped bring justice and dignity to the farmworkers.

This is a historic day.

The contract gave workers a minimum wage of $1.80 an hour plus 20 cents for each box of grapes. It also guaranteed health benefits, retirement funding, and banned certain pesticide use that was unsafe for workers' health.

We said from the beginning that we were not going to abandon the fight, that we would stay with the struggle if it took a lifetime, and we meant it!

The strike had been a long journey. But the victory was due to the hard work of many people coming together.

With a contract in place, the Manongs returned to work—but not all was what they hoped for. Each day, many would wait in line at the Union Hiring Hall for their job assignments, only to be turned away.

We have no shifts remaining for you. Try again tomorrow.

After years of fighting, the new contract still didn't provide for the migrant workers. Because the Manongs always traveled for work, they were passed over for "more senior" local Mexican American workers.

For Larry Itliong, being a part of the UFW had been incredibly challenging. During and after the strike, press coverage focused more on Chávez and the Mexican participants, while Itliong and the Filipinos were ignored.

With his role and influence shrinking, Itliong quit the UFW in 1971. In his resignation letter, he noted how the Filipino members of the union had no voice.

identity to the ...eship. Altho many broader sp... involed themselves to remedy the bad situition faced by our people, no oratory or pleading of the minority leadership ~~wit~~ within the leadership. Can convince the majority that if we pull ourselves together, we can be a lot stronger and more effective.

Still, Itliong never gave up on the Manongs. Before his death in 1977, he helped develop a retirement home for Filipino workers and made public appearances to support their rights.

And in 2015, nearly 100 years after the first Filipino workers arrived in California, Governor Jerry Brown signed a bill proclaiming October 25 Larry Itliong Day.

Larry Itliong's legacy continues to inspire the next generation of leaders across California and the nation.

As for the members of the UFW, their work didn't end with the first workers' contract in 1970. In the many years since, the union has continued to fight for all farmworkers.

In the mid-1970s, the UFW won contracts with lettuce growers in California and citrus growers in Florida.

We will not stop fighting, until all workers are protected!

By the early 1980s, UFW contracts covered more than 40,000 farmworkers. But Chávez continued his work—sometimes using hunger strikes—to raise awareness of the dangers of pesticides.

Together we will confront and resist with all of our strength the scourge of poisons that threaten our people and our land and our food.

Even today, the fight started by Itliong, Chávez, Huerta, and so many others continues on.

Whether protecting workers from rising temperatures due to climate change or fighting for their rights during a devastating global pandemic . . .

. . . the UFW and other unions are committed to ensuring American farm laborers are paid fairly and treated with the dignity they deserve.

MORE ABOUT THE DELANO GRAPE STRIKE

- In 1965, the average annual income for an American worker was $4,658.72. Farmworkers were making about half of that, $50 a week or $2,600 a year.

- Before the Delano Grape Strike, farmworkers negotiated pay at the start of each season, asking for a little more than the previous year. One result of the strike was that contracts began including year-over-year wage increases.

- Larry Itliong and César Chávez had very different perspectives on organizing tactics. Itliong was okay with meeting aggression from growers with aggression. The Coachella strike involved instances of violence between growers and strikers, which led to its resolution. Chávez preferred nonviolent tactics.

- In 1968, when Chávez learned there were plans for Filipino and Mexican strikers to increase aggression, he began a fast—drinking only water for 25 days as a commitment to peaceful protest. Some in the union thought Chávez was doing it as stunt to boost his image. However, it did raise awareness of the overall strike.

- Twenty-five percent of grape farms in California did not sign the initial contract in 1970. As a result, UFW kept striking at those farms. The union also created a label to mark union grapes. It encouraged shoppers to continue supporting the laborers.

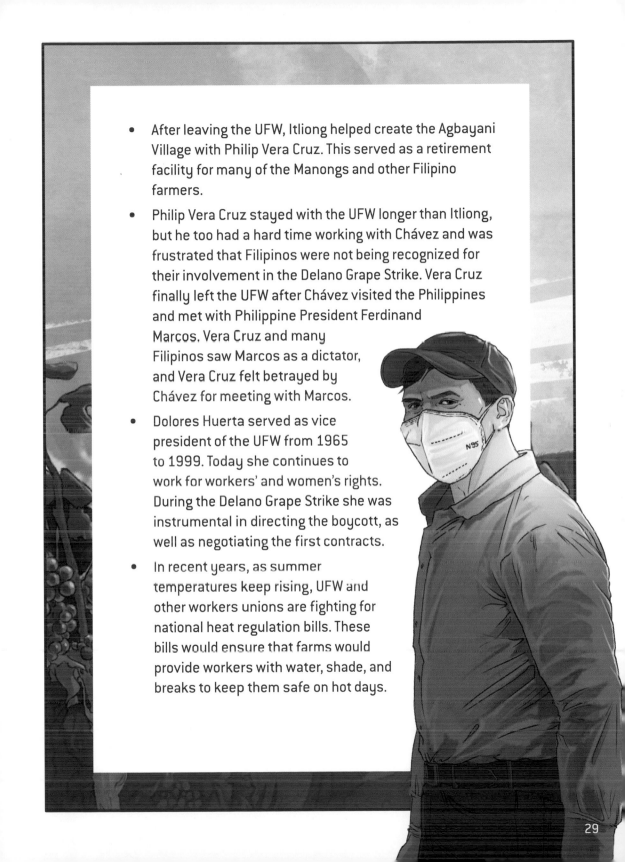

- After leaving the UFW, Itliong helped create the Agbayani Village with Philip Vera Cruz. This served as a retirement facility for many of the Manongs and other Filipino farmers.

- Philip Vera Cruz stayed with the UFW longer than Itliong, but he too had a hard time working with Chávez and was frustrated that Filipinos were not being recognized for their involvement in the Delano Grape Strike. Vera Cruz finally left the UFW after Chávez visited the Philippines and met with Philippine President Ferdinand Marcos. Vera Cruz and many Filipinos saw Marcos as a dictator, and Vera Cruz felt betrayed by Chávez for meeting with Marcos.

- Dolores Huerta served as vice president of the UFW from 1965 to 1999. Today she continues to work for workers' and women's rights. During the Delano Grape Strike she was instrumental in directing the boycott, as well as negotiating the first contracts.

- In recent years, as summer temperatures keep rising, UFW and other workers unions are fighting for national heat regulation bills. These bills would ensure that farms would provide workers with water, shade, and breaks to keep them safe on hot days.

GLOSSARY

boycott (BOY-kot)—to stop buying something to show support for an idea or group of people

contract (KAHN-trakt)—an agreement to do something

discrimination (dis-krih-muh-NAY-shuhn)—treating people unfairly because of their race, country of birth, gender, or other categories of identity

generation (jen-uh-RAY-shuhn)—a group of people born around the same time

immigrant (IMM-uh-gruhnt)—a person who moves from a country with the intention to live permanently in another country

migrant (MYE-gruhnt)—a person who moves to a new area or country, generally in search of work

negotiation (nih-goh-shee-AY-shuhn)—talking to reach an agreement

pesticide (PESS-tuh-side)—a poisonous chemical used to kill insects, rats, and fungi that can damage plants

picket (PIK-it)—to stand outside a place to spread your message

plantation (plan-TAY-shuhn)—a large farm where crops such as cotton and sugarcane are grown; before 1865, plantations were run by enslaved people

scab (SKAB)—someone who takes the job of a union worker who is on strike

strike (STRIKE)—to refuse to work because of a disagreement with the employer over wages or working conditions

unanimous (yoo-NAN-uh-muhss)—agreed on by everyone

union (YOON-yuhn)—a group of workers who try to gain more rights, such as fair pay and safer jobs, for workers

READ MORE

Mattern, Joanne. *César Chávez: Labor Rights Activist.* New York: Cavendish Square Publishing, 2020.

Moening, Kate. *Dolores Huerta: Labor Activist.* Minneapolis: Bellwether Media, 2020.

Zilka, Rose. *Larry Itliong Leads the Way for Farmworkers' Rights.* Lake Elmo, MN: Focus Readers, 2019.

INTERNET SITES

The 1965–1970 Delano Grape Strike and Boycott
ufw.org/1965-1970-delano-grape-strike-boycott

Delano Grape Strike and Boycott, 1965: Records of Rights
recordsofrights.org/events/43/delano-grape-strike-and-boycott

Delano Manongs
pbs.org/video/kvie-viewfinder-delano-manongs

ABOUT THE AUTHOR

 Daniel Mauleón earned an MFA in Writing for Children and Young Adults at Hamline University in 2017. Since then, he has written fiction, nonfiction, and graphic novels for Capstone. He lives in Minneapolis with his wife and two cats.

ABOUT THE ILLUSTRATOR

 János Orbán grew up in Budapest, Hungary, where his love of art began at an early age. After graduating from an art high school, he went on to earn a degree from the Hungarian University of Fine Arts. With a passion for illustration, Orbán most enjoys designing characters and creating artwork for children's books. He has two daughters and a son, and he currently lives and works with his family in a village near Budapest.